# YOUR KNOWLEDGE HAS VALUE

- We will publish your bachelor's and master's thesis, essays and papers

- Your own eBook and book - sold worldwide in all relevant shops

- Earn money with each sale

Upload your text at www.GRIN.com and publish for free

**Bibliographic information published by the German National Library:**

The German National Library lists this publication in the National Bibliography; detailed bibliographic data are available on the Internet at http://dnb.dnb.de .



**Imprint:**

Copyright © 2012 GRIN Verlag, Open Publishing GmbH
Print and binding: Books on Demand GmbH, Norderstedt Germany
ISBN: 9783668265417

**This book at GRIN:**

http://www.grin.com/en/e-book/193126/buck-summer-summers-on-the-lonely-isle

Kirby Wright

# Buck Summer. Summers on the Lonely Isle

GRIN Publishing

## BUCK SUMMER

It was a kill my grandmother would have hated—multiple shots through a sniper's scope across the mile breadth of Kainalu Valley. "Bloody coward," I imagined Gramma saying. She felt a hunter should give a buck a fighting chance by firing only one shot through open sites within one hundred yards. My big brother Ben had just fired five times at a buck on the opposite ridge and now it was lying on its side in a clearing. He'd let me shoot too, just for fun, through the open sites of his old .22.

I picked up two brass casings Ben's rifle had ejected—they were still warm. The air smelled of gunpowder, the scent of celebration. It was the same acrid firecracker odor that lingered in the islands every July Fourth, New Year, and Chinese New Year.

Ben studied the buck through his .270's scope. His blond hair glinted like gold. The hairs on his neck and arms were blond too. Gramma called him a "sissy" because he had our Irish mother's looks. I took after our *hapa haole* father with my dark complexion and rugged features. Strangers didn't think we were brothers at all.

"Big horns?" I asked.

Ben shifted the butt of the rifle so it rested lower down on his shoulder. "Not bad," he said. "Can't find the entry wound."

"Where'd you aim?"

"His chest."

"Maybe he's bluffing."

"Bluffing, my ass," Ben told me. He lowered his .270 and cradled it in his arms. The wooden stock glowed like honey and its black barrel was shiny from oilings. Ben picked his nose. "No buck lies on his side like that," he told me.

Ben had been trying to shoot his first buck all summer. It was something he could tell all his Diamond Head pals back home in Honolulu, boys he considered losers for idling away their summers surfing, smoking *pakalolo*, and chasing after girls at the Kahala Hilton. The only friend he respected was a *popolo* boy named Barry who had a summer job selling hotdogs off a cart in Waikiki.

"Bet Barry's making planny *kala*," Ben had said.

"How much can you make selling hotdogs?" I'd asked.

He'd chuckled. "That's not all he sells."

My brother was determined to start sophomore year at Punahou School with another trophy hanging off his bedroom wall. He thought of himself as the De Niro character in *The Deer Hunter*, a crack shot sportsman with a cool head and a hoard of idiot friends. Everything he was wearing today was camouflage: shirt, pants, and even a cap. He'd bought the outfit at Big 88 Surplus in Honolulu, along with an olive-colored plastic canteen and a matching belt. A Buck knife and a hatchet hung in leather sheaths attached to the belt. Gramma had told me Ben's outfit was "silly business" and that "the Prince of Wales couldn't hit the side of a barn." This was our ninth straight summer on our grandmother's *ahupua'a*, a 250-acre ranch starting at the shore and reaching up to the skyline. The ranch was an ancient Hawaiian land division that recognized the sacred elements of land, water, and sky.

*      *      *

I followed Ben down through wild guava and mountain apple trees. The .270 swayed on a sling off his right shoulder. His Army boots left deep tracks. The ground was muddy from a recent rain so I held on to the branches to steady myself. I had on a t-shirt, swim trunks, and Keds. The day pack slung over my left shoulder contained a pair of binoculars, a skinning knife, laundry cord, and burlap bags. The knife was rolled up in the burlap to prevent the blade from stabbing me. The barrel of the .22 poked out of the top of the pack.

Ben took a narrow trail covered with ti plants. He didn't look back to see if I was keeping up. It was as if he wanted to reach his kill in the shortest possible time and it didn't matter if I fell behind. I followed a path of crushed ti. He sidestepped the thick trunk of a koa and examined a mound of droppings that resembled Chinese black beans.

Ben crouched. "Goat," he said.

I dropped to one knee. There was the aroma of fresh-cut grass.

"Wanna shoot one?" he asked.

"No."

"How come?"

"I dunno," I said.

"You dunno 'cause you're chicken."

"We don't eat goat meat."

"The dogs will. That'll save money on canned food."

"But the dogs love their Friskies."

Ben shook his head. "If you don't start shooting soon, Jeffo, you'll never be a hunter."

"I'd rather be a fisherman."

"Fishing's for wimps," he told me.

"What about sharks?"

"What about 'em?"

"What if you spear a hammerhead like Daddy?"

"What if, what if," he mimicked. "What if the rabbit hadn't stopped?"

Now Ben was using our grandmother's "what if" chiding against me. It was as if Gramma was on the hunt with us. It made me feel like a baby.

Ben stood. He adjusted the sling on his rifle. "I was two years younger than you when I shot my first billy," he said. "You've gotta make this your goat summer."

"Should I use the .22?"

"I'll let you borrow my .270 when I sniff one."

"They stink?"

"Billies pee on themselves to turn on the nannies. Imagine if we had to pee on ourselves to get chicks?"

"I'd never do it."

He smirked. "You'd take pee showers if you knew it'd turn on Debbie Mills."

"I don't like Debbie."

"Liar," he replied. "You'd fuck her like a horny rabbit."

Ben's goat head hung off his bedroom wall back home in Honolulu. He always invited boys into his room to look at it. Most were impressed. He'd fired three .22 hollow points into the billy's back but the billy ran into a ravine and it took Ben all day tracking the blood. He'd finally found it breathing heavy under a fern—that's when he pulled his knife. The billy didn't impress Gramma. In her hierarchy of hunting, the goat was below the lowly pig.

"*Hum ha*," Gramma had scolded him, "get outta my house."

"What for?" he'd asked.

"You stink like a god damned goat."

*        *        *

Ben skirted a hill of boulders and eased through the timber bamboo. Green stalks spiked into the sky. The bamboo was shedding and we trudged over brown soggy leaves. I followed Ben down to the valley floor, where the pungent sweet of mango rose up. I could hear water cascading in the gorge. I wanted to hike up, wade through the pool, and stand under the showering falls.

Ben leaned his .270 against the trunk of an ohia tree and sat on a stone ledge. "Take five," he said.

I took off my pack and sat beside him.

A mango tree formed a canopy that shaded the middle valley. Doves cooed in its branches. Dots of light freckled the lavender bamboo orchids growing beneath the tree. A breeze from the ocean rustled the leaves, making the light dance. I was glad for the time-out. It seemed as though we were on a simple hike and not tracking something dead on Dunbar Ridge. The valley was humid. My tee was drenched so I pulled it off and wrung out the sweat. "How old's the mango tree?" I asked Ben.

He stretched out his arms and yawned. "As old as King Kamehameha."

"Do you think Daddy ate any of its mangoes, when he was a boy?"

"The General probably ate the green ones and got diarrhea," Ben said. He'd started calling our father "the General" because he loved giving orders. Ben had put his fists up to him trying to defend our mother and received a black eye for his trouble—he hid the bruise under foundation powder he found in my mother's bathroom.

"Time to *hele*," Ben said.

I pulled my t-shirt over my head, picked up my pack, and followed Ben east. Fruit flies buzzed a fallen mango while a myna bird gobbled up the spattered pulp. We hopped from boulder to boulder, then jumped over a stream surging past a shore of stones. The water was clear and bubbly.

Ben led the way up Dunbar Ridge. We weren't supposed to be here. Gramma's property ended at the stream but Ben figured Dunbar was too busy getting drunk on *okolehao* in the flatlands to care. Sheer lava cliffs blotted out the sun. We took a switchback trail that wove through the trees. It was so steep we grabbed one trunk after the next, pulling ourselves up. I knew Ben would tack this struggle on to his buck story and bank it away deep inside. He could visit that bank whenever our grandmother got under his skin by comparing him to our old man. As a boy, our father had lived in Honolulu during the school year and visited Moloka'i every summer. Gramma's stories about his *keiko o ka aina* exploits seemed more mythical that real, especially the ones about him spearing hammerhead sharks, swimming the seven miles of Pailolo Channel to Maui, and roping wild horses. Ben said the stories were "bullshit" but they still inspired him. "What great thing am I going to do today?" Ben would ask Gramma and she'd reply, "not a bloody god damn thing." He'd nearly murdered a poacher with his .22 the previous summer and he fired at trespassers whenever he saw them hiking our mountain. Gramma'd told Ben cowards used guns instead of fists and he retaliated by saying she didn't have the courage to raise her own son.

The switchback ended and the ridge flattened out. We hustled through a web of ferns—we reached a clearing filled with sour grass, lantana, and fireweed. No sign of the buck.

Ben pulled up his rifle. He stared through his scope across the valley, at the ridge where we'd camped. "That was some shot," he said.

"Shots," I replied.

Ben rolled his eyes. "One shot or a hundred," he said, "it's all the same if the target's dead."

I gazed up at the mountains: small trunks with leafless branches dotted an emerald meadow that rolled up to the sky. Gramma had told me she heard ghost drums pounding near a trail that disappeared into the mist.

"Head south and I'll go north," Ben told me.

"Which way's south?" I asked.

"Toward the ocean, dummy. Keep an eye on Brownie's Gulch so you don't go too far."

He headed toward the skyline.

I walked the opposite way. Pailolo Channel glimmered between the ridges, its blue so dark it looked cobalt.  Shark water.  I searched the base of a Cooke pine and wandered through plum trees.  A yellow orchid grew beside a fern.  I sucked at the air through my nose—I smelled the stinky mud on the flats west of the harbor.  I wanted to be there with my rod and reel, casting for barracuda in the whitewater behind the barrier reef.  I always fished alone.  I'd think a lot about Debbie Mills and wondered if I could somehow find the courage to ask her out.  Ben wasn't much of a role model when it came to girls.  He was still harboring a crush on a cheerleader.  He hadn't spoken a word to her in two years because she'd shot him down when he asked her to go with him to the Punahou Carnival.  At least I'd danced with Debbie Mills at 8$^{th}$ Grade Canteen.

"*Hui!*" Ben called.

I darted through the plum trees and jogged the clearing.  The sour grass and fireweed stung my bare legs.  I found Ben kneeling beside an ohia tree, his rifle hanging off a branch.  The buck was on its side with its legs splayed.

"How'd he get here?" I asked Ben.

"Musta crawled," he replied.

"Is he dead?"

Ben held his palm against the buck's chest.  "Zero heartbeat."

I knelt down.  The hide was rust brown with white spots.  A white patch ran from under his neck to his chest.  He was beautiful.  I remembered watching through binoculars as the buck moved slowly through the clearing before stopping to graze.  Two does were with him.  One of the does turned her head and stared at us on our perch above Brownie's Gulch.  That's when Ben fired.  I fired too.  I was surprised the does stayed with the buck after his legs buckled.  We kept firing and the barrage drove away the does.  I hated myself for shooting.  But Gramma had told us we "couldn't hold a candle to Buddy" and I wanted to prove her wrong about us being tenderfoots compared to our father.  Killing a buck and packing it down would at least end her complaint we couldn't put meat on the table.  I wanted to string the deer up on the hanging tree and have her watch us gut it through the beach house window.

I ran my hand over the hide.  It felt like the hair on a dog.  I touched his black nose—it was cold and dry.  He was only a little bigger than Gramma's German Shepherd.  His antlers were not impressive and I wondered if the scope made them appear larger, the way a diving mask exaggerates the size of fish. Ben finally had his buck but I doubted it would impress our grandmother.

I found a tiny hole in the neck. "Is this the entry wound?" I asked.

Ben dug his finger in the hole, pulled it out, and sniffed. "Smells like steel," he said.

"Isn't that hole too small for a .270?"

"Bullet fragged." He grabbed an antler and twisted the head. "Fuck," he said, "only one horn."

A black, bone-like stump was where the other antler should have been. That made the buck look even smaller.

"Holy shit," I said, "how'd he lose it?"

"Who the hell cares how he lost it," Ben replied. "That bitch's going to have a field day with me."

"Who cares what Gramma thinks."

"I do."

"At least we have venison," I said.

Ben flipped the buck on its backside. "Bring my rifle."

I grabbed the .270 and followed as he dragged the buck to the edge of the clearing. Then we started down Dunbar Ridge. Ben found a new path through the ohia trees, one with a steeper decline that made dragging easy. There were tiny ferns under the trees that Ben crushed dragging the carcass. The path turned to lava and we reached the edge of the ridge.

"End of the bloody road," Ben said.

I held onto a koa trunk and peered over: the valley was a straight drop down. A tiny falls trickled off the cliff's face. I couldn't see the bottom because pines crowded the ravine below. I shifted the .270 to my right shoulder, picked up a rock, and tossed it over. The rock disappeared into the pine and clinked on the valley floor. "Gotta find that switchback," I said.

"What for?" Ben asked.

"To pack the buck down safely."

"I'm not dragging this bastard any farther," he said.

"What if I help?"

He sat down, bent his knees, and placed his boots on the buck's rear. He pushed. The lava sandpapered the hide. Ben kept pushing with his legs and scrooching behind until the antler dangled over the edge. Sweat beaded up on my brother's forehead and he wiped it away with the back of his hand. A crease formed between his eyebrows. He swallowed hard. His green eyes looked angry.

"Don't do it," I told him.

"Why the fuck not?"

"You'll ruin the meat."

"Bombs away," he snickered, jamming his boots into the rump.

The buck went over. He flipped in mid-air, smashed into a lava outcropping, and disappeared in the trees. I heard a thud-thud-thud on the valley floor and pictured the body tumbling. I felt defeated. We'd made the hike from Brownie's Gulch into the valley and crossed over but, in the end, had to cheat to get the buck off Dunbar Ridge. Men didn't toss deer off cliffs. If Gramma found out she'd never let us hunt again.

"Gimmee back my rifle," Ben groused.

*      *      *

We retraced our steps to the clearing. Ben found the switchback and carved a path through the ferns and trees like a fullback powering through a field of sloppy tacklers. We hung onto ohia branches to slow ourselves down—I accidentally snapped off a branch with red lehua flowers. We reached bottom and skirted the edge of Dunbar Ridge. Ben gazed up through the trees and spotted the tiny falls. We hiked through the pines. A watering hole glistened between two Norfolks. I found the buck sprawled on a nest of ferns. Except for a compound fracture to his front leg you'd never know he'd fallen. His brown eyes were open and it appeared as if mascara had been applied to the lids. His antler was still intact.

I poked the hindquarter with my thumb. "Mushy," I told Ben.

"Let's pack 'im down anyway," he said. "Grab the back legs, I'll take the front."

"Shouldn't we gut 'im first?"

"We'll do that later."

Ben hiked face forward, with his hands behind him holding the front legs at the knee joint.  I brought up the rear, my fingers wrapped around the hooves.  We entered a tree fern forest growing beside the stream.  The fronds rose thirty feet.  It was hard packing the buck down through the valley because of the boulders, the ferns, and the stream.  Mosquitoes came out of the half-light and swarmed us.  The .270 fell off Ben's shoulder and splashed in the stream—he dropped his half of the buck reaching for the gun.

"Stupe," he called himself, pouring water out of the barrel.

We kept going.  My fingers ached holding up the hooves.  The tree ferns thinned out and the sky opened.  I caught a whiff of the pig farm that was tucked behind the public road at the valley's mouth.  Kiawe trees covered the lower valley.  There was more sunlight here because the kiawe leaves were tiny.  Lilikoi wrapped their vines around the kiawe trunks and branches, their yellow balls of passion fruit dangling like Christmas ornaments.

We followed the stonewall the *piha kanaka maoli* had built to designate districts in the time of kings.  The wall was eight feet high and its stones were covered with lime-green lichens.  I imagined Hawaiian men passing stones hand to hand from the shore up into the valley.  Gramma owned everything east of the wall and Dunbar owned all the rest.

We reached our first ironwood and Ben stopped.  "Put 'im down," he said, lowering the deer.

I put my side on the ground.  "Take five?"

"Take five, nothing.  We're deboning 'im."

"What?"

"Read about it in *Field & Stream*.  We get rid of all the bone and pack only the meat.  Then we don't have to string him up at the beach house."

I was disappointed.  I wanted to butcher the deer in front of our grandmother to show her we weren't scared of getting our hands bloody.  "A hunter packs the whole deer down," I told my brother.

"Who says?"

"Gramma."

He pulled out his Buck knife—it had a 10-inch blade.  "She's full of shit," he snapped. "Gimmee some cord."

I fished around inside my pack. I found the roll of laundry cord and tossed it to him.

Ben cut two lengths off the cord and stabbed the ironwood's trunk hard enough to make the blade stick. He made slipknots, looped the knotted cord around the front and back hooves, and tossed the ends over a limb. "Heave ho," he said.

I grabbed the cord binding the rear hooves. We hoisted the buck off the ground but the rump dangled only a few feet above a bed of ironwood needles. The body swung at an angle, the front higher up than the rear.

"Higher," Ben told me.

I pulled but the cord slipped through my hands, burning my fingers and palms.

"Be a dead weight and just hang on the cord," Ben said, lowering his side. "We go on three."

I wrapped my hands around the cord.

"One," he said, "two, three!"

I leaned back, letting the cord hold me up. The buck rose and dangled at eye level. The neck twisted down. The tip of the antler touched ground—it carved through the ironwood needles as the body swayed.

Ben tied his end of the rope to a branch while I square-knotted my side to a kiawe stump.

Ben pulled his hatchet out of its sheath. "First things first."

"Guttin' 'im?" I asked.

"Taking off his head."

"Better bleed 'im before the meat spoils."

"It's my buck," he answered. "I'll do what I want." He held the hatchet like a bat, swinging at the neck. The blade hit the shoulder but bounced off. He swung a second time and again it bounced. "Just going to stand there with your finger up your *okole*?" Ben asked me.

"No."

"Good. Start skinning."

I grabbed my pack. My face burned and my hands shook. I hated my brother

when he got like this.  I heard him hack-hack-hacking, trying to break through the bone.
He was more mean than kind and the meanness was growing as he got older.  I pulled out
a burlap bag and unwrapped the skinning knife.  The blade was short.  I dragged it over
my forearm and shaved off a patch of hair.  I made incisions in the hide around a back
hoof and then slipped the knife under the hide, blade facing out.  I cut vertically to the
knee joint, continued on to the hindquarter, and grabbed the loose hide at the hoof.  I
peeled down.  The hide made a vacuum sound as it separated from the meat.  There were
blood pockets where the venison was bruised—it would taste mushy after Gramma
cooked it.  Maybe she'd toss it to the dogs.  I finished peeling the hide off the first leg and
started in on the other.  I'd learned watching hunters butcher deer, goats, and pigs on the
hanging tree.  A hunter named Eckman had given me his Nazi dagger and coached me as
I sliced through his boar.  Men seemed to like it when boys bloodied their hands.

"Look," Ben said.

I glanced over—Ben held the head by the antler.  Blood spilled out of the neck,
splattering his boots.  "Buck's head soup," he chuckled.

"Going to mount it?" I asked.

He shook his head.  "That'd be a waste with only one horn."  He placed the head
in the crotch of the ironwood.  He swung the hatchet, lodged it in the trunk, and pulled
his knife out of the tree.  The steel glinted in the sun.  He slid his blade into the deer's
chest and worked his way down the torso.  The knife ripped easily through the cartilage.

The sound made me queasy.  I finished cutting the second hindquarter.  I peeled
down to the ribs.  The hide looked like a jacket turned inside out.  "How's it going?" I
asked Ben.

"Okay.  Blade needs sharpening."

Blood pooled on the ironwood needles.  Ben split open the belly and the entrails
spilled out.  It smelled like horse manure mixed with fermented ferns and fruit.

"Can you guess why I picked this tree?" Ben asked.

"It's like the hanging tree."

He nodded.  "Gramma doesn't like us, you know.  She thinks we're sissies."

"Sissies don't shoot and pack bucks," I said.

Ben stuck the knife in the ground.  He pulled the hatchet out of the trunk and hacked at the hips. He broke through and retrieved his knife. "Filet time," he said and started carving. The meat fell away in slabs and landed on the needles.

I picked up a slab and plucked off the needles. The meat felt slimy. I stuffed it into a burlap bag. Above me, the bones gleamed white as bleached coral. Blooms of flesh clung to the ribs. I filled one bag and started in on another.

Ben severed the balls and penis. He dropped the balls but held the penis in his hand. He rolled the penis back and forth between his palm and fingers. It was covered with white fur and reminded me of a rabbit's foot. "Won't be needing this anymore," Ben said. He tossed the penis into the stream. The water carried it south toward the flatlands. He washed the knife and hatchet in the stream and put them back in their sheaths.

"At least we're bringing home meat," I told Ben.

"Too bad the venison's spoiled," he said.

"Might be *ono* if I soak it in soy sauce."

"It'll taste like blood pudding."

"What if we barbecue it?" I asked.

"That won't help."

"Can we give it to the Duvas? Or Dan Naki?"

"Those *kanakas* can suck eggs."

"Just leave the meat?"

Ben nodded. "Let the mongoose have it." He pulled the head out of the tree and ran his fingers over the antler. "Guess one horn's better than none," he said.

"Can I cut down the bones?" I asked.

"Leave 'em."

"And the cord?"

"Cord's no good once blood hits it." He walked downstream holding the head by the antler, his .270 slung off his right shoulder. He was coming out of the wilderness with a buck, even though he knew Gramma would make fun of him. "Fo' chrissakes," I could hear her laughing, "wheah's the othah bloody horn?"

I look at the bags. The meat bled through the burlap. Flies circled the bones. One landed on the shattered hip and rubbed its wings together. The stench of butchering made me nauseous.  I fought it off.  I wanted to bring back venison to show Gramma that my brother was a good hunter.  But I knew that wouldn't work.  A wall like the one dividing the valley had formed between my grandmother and Ben.  The stones in the wall were not made out of coral or lava.  They were fashioned from hatred, guilt, and shame, weight my grandmother lugged year after year for not raising her son.  Now, sick of Ben's challenging nature, she was using those stones and making new ones to wall herself off from him.  The wall grew stronger every summer and I wanted to tear it down. But it was already too late.

**<u>Notes:</u>**

*hapa haole*: part Hawaiian and part white

*pakalolo*: marijuana

*popolo*: black

*kala*: money

*ahupua'a*: Hawaiian land division

*hum ha*: shrimp paste with putrid odor

*hele*: go

*okolehao*: liquor made from fermented ti root

*keiki o ka aina*: child of the land and the sea

*hui*: hello

*piha kanaka maoli*: having 100% Hawaiian blood

*okole*: butt

*ono*: tasty

*kanaka*: derogatory term word for Hawaiian man

# YOUR KNOWLEDGE HAS VALUE

- We will publish your bachelor's and master's thesis, essays and papers

- Your own eBook and book - sold worldwide in all relevant shops

- Earn money with each sale

Upload your text at www.GRIN.com and publish for free